Because

there's COLOR in a black & white world

Because
there's COLOR in a black & white world

Maria Magistro and Meg Schutte

**Andrews McMeel
Publishing**

Kansas City

02 03 04 05 06 TWP 10 9 8 7 6 5 4 3 2 1

ISBN: 0-7407-2897-0

Library of Congress Control Number: 2002103778

Attention: Schools and Businesses
Andrews McMeel books are available at quantity discounts with bulk purchase for educational, business, or sales promotional use. For information, please write to: Special Sales Department, Andrews McMeel Publishing, 4520 Main Street, Kansas City, Missouri 64111.

Because

there's COLOR in a black & white world

Sometimes in observing one small gesture
you can know someone completely

Radiance knows no age

Good breeding just shows

The art of doing nothing is really something

We each have our own place in the world

Horizons change and so do we

Strong spirits stand tall

You are who you are who you are . . .

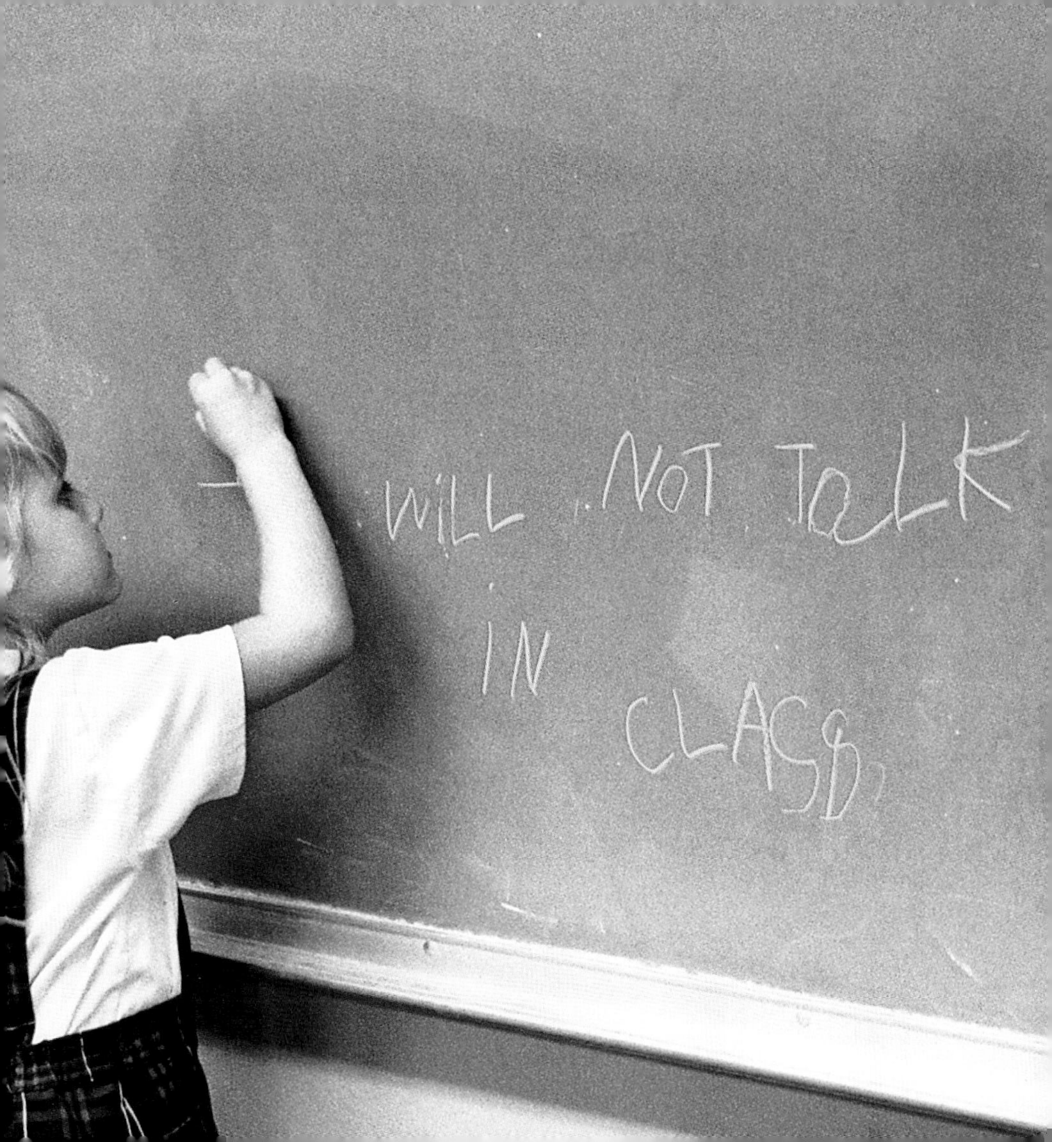
WILL NOT TALK
IN
CLASS

Charming is as charming does

Once a princess always a princess

Inside each of us is a great idea

Sometimes it's good just to be in the moment

Good friends see the world the same way

The best things in life are often right in front of us

In truth . . . they've all been good years

The good life is how you live it

Every love has a story of how it came to be

Somewhere there is a puddle waiting for you

Both courage and fear dwell in the heart of a hero

You can count the years or celebrate them

With every ending comes a new beginning

Thinking big has its own rewards

Always lead with your assets

AS ADVERTISED
ANTALOUPE
39¢ LB.

Freedom can come in the smallest ways

When there's nowhere else you'd rather be you've found the one

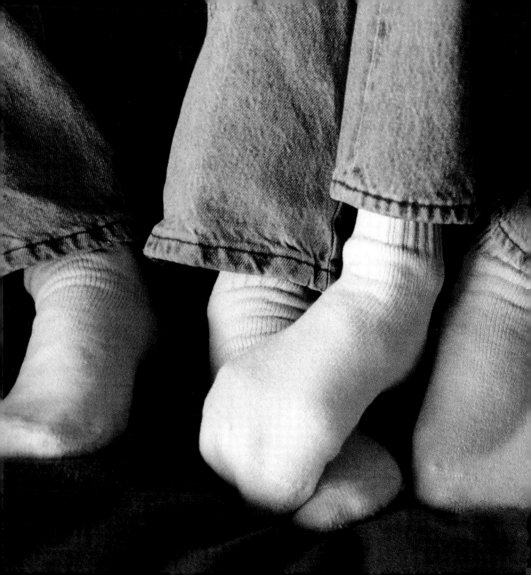

We each create the life we were meant to live

How you see the world says a lot about you

Just think, it could have been worse

Write yourself a happy ending

A Special Thanks To:

Man and dog on bench: Heather Jean and Louis Maniscalco
Dog with gift: Ginger
Cat with vase: Pooka
Girl at chalkboard: Cheyenne Henley
Woman with rubber gloves: Andrea
Dog with beret: Axle
Cat with computer: Pooka
Kids with goggles: Maddy and Alex Schoenberger
Dog with treats: Kodi
Dog on bench: Bogart
Couple's hands: Irene Schuster and Rev. John Weaver
Girl with rain boots: Maddy Schoenberger
Dog with life jacket: Foley
Baby with ribbons: Lila Nelson
Woman with melons: Rose Maniscalco
Legs in jeans: Greg and Susan Merrill
Bowl of oranges: Elise's kitchen
Sand castle: Nancy's creation
Gum on shoe: Jon Nadler